Amish

Crib Quilts

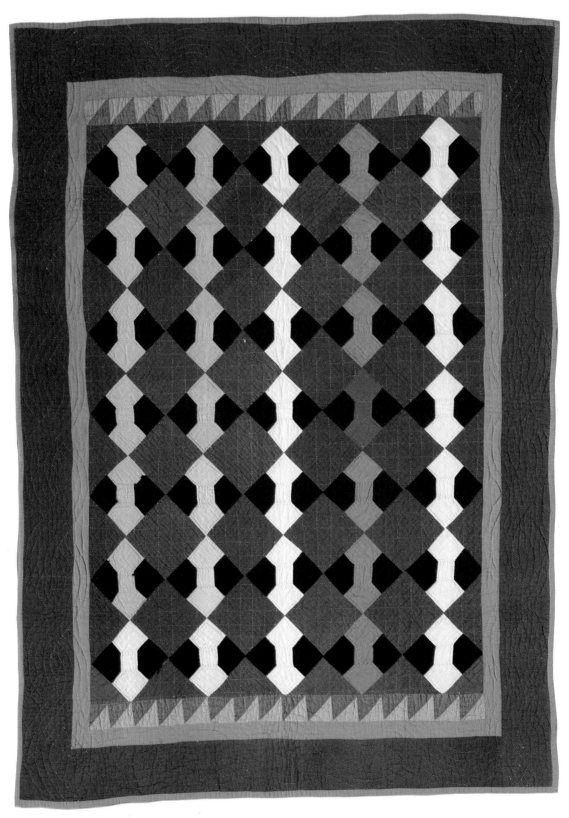

Bow Ties. c. 1930–40. Cotton. 38 × 54. Middlefield. Ohio. Collection of Eve and David Wheatcroft. Lewisburg. PA. Bright little bow ties stand out sharply against their black negative space. Note the subtle variations in the shade of the background fabrics.

Amish
Crib Quilts

Rachel and Kenneth Pellman

Good Books
Intercourse, Pennsylvania 17534

On The Covers

Log Cabin—Straight Furrows variation, c. 1920–30. Cotton sateen, wool, 30 × 42. Holmes Co., Ohio. Collection of Eve and David Wheatcroft, Lewisburg, PA. Quilting on the outer border of this quilt continues the theme of straight diagonal lines.

Baskets, c. 1910. Wool, 33 × 42. Holmes Co., Ohio. Collection of Eve and David Wheatcroft, Lewisburg, PA. Tiny stacked triangles form baskets to fill the interior of this quilt while full quilted fans adorn the border.

Acknowledgments

Design by Craig N. Heisey

We wish to express our gratitude to the many friends who kindly permitted us to exhibit their treasured quilts on the following pages. We are also pleased with the way Kirk Zutell captured these wonderful masterpieces on film. We are grateful to the dozens and dozens of Amish folks from near and far who provided us with invaluable information about Amish life and crib quilts.

We are also delighted to include the stories and poetry from *Family Life* and *Blackboard Bulletin.* We have been warmed by the help and cooperation of so many persons. Thanks.

Photograph Credits

Cover Photo: Kirk Zutell/BRT Photographic Illustrations
All photos throughout the book were taken by Kirk Zutell/BRT Photographic Illustrations except the following:
Bill Coleman, 1, 8, 22, 57, 72, 82; Kenneth Pellman, 5, 31; David Lauver, 11, 32, 46, 92; Richard Reinhold, 13, 91; Jerry Irwin, 17, 26, 62, 66, 77, 86; Blair Seitz, 37, 42, 51, 52, 71.

Amish Crib Quilts
Copyright © 1985 by Good Books, Intercourse, PA 17534
International Standard Book Number: 0-934672-29-6
Library of Congress Catalog Card Number: 85-70281

Amish
Crib Quilts

Contents

Introduction to Amish Crib Quilts

Amish crib quilts mirror full-size quilts in much the same way as Amish children are miniature copies of Amish adults. What is it that sets these quilts—and people—apart? There is strength in their families, communities and churches. And there is strength in the juxtaposition of deeply hued jewel colors common in Amish quilts. There is simplicity in these people's dress and lifestyle that is echoed in the restraint of their bold geometric quilt patterns. And discipline is a value that the Amish apply to children, adults and quilts alike.

Antique (pre-1940) Amish crib quilts are generally of the same patterns that appear in full-size antique Amish quilts. For the most part they are designs employed by quiltmakers everywhere, not just Amish women. However, there are several patterns unique to Amish quilts. The Center Diamond can often be traced to roots in eastern Pennsylvania. The Bars pattern appears predominately in Pennsylvania Amish quilts but is found on occasion among midwestern Amish groups as well. Sunshine and Shadow is used in Amish settlements throughout North America. Amish women in midwestern states generally used a wider variety of patterns in their quiltmaking. However, the feeling of restraint is still there.

Quilts were first and primarily a functional item. Whole cloth tops and pieced tops of simple geometric shapes were acceptable. But appliquéing on antique Amish quilts is extremely rare because that was thought to be showy and extravagant.

All these principles follow through to antique Amish crib quilts. In some cases, the same patterns were used but reduced in scale to produce a lovely miniature of the larger quilt. In other cases, the scale of the pattern was not changed, so that the size of the individual patches, though appropriate for a full-size quilt, can seem overpowering in a crib quilt. Although the proportions of these quilts are not always as pleasing as full-size quilts, their bold colors and muted energy make them dramatic examples of Amish quiltmaking. As in the larger quilts, crib quilts almost always have their pieced patterns contained within strong borders which seem to restrain even the most exuberant quilt.

Unique and Dynamic Color

What sets antique Amish quilts apart more than any other single factor is their color. These quilts were made using fabrics of only solid colors. And those colors are, for the most part, limited to the colors of Amish clothing. The result is a bold assemblage of deep, vivid hues which seem in some instances joyful and aggressive, while in other cases somber and withdrawn. In fact, when viewing these vibrant quilts, one wonders how a child was expected to sleep! They are stimulating, exciting pieces. Pastel pinks and blues were not the mode for Amish quiltmakers. There seems to be little difference in the colors of full-size quilts and their smaller counterparts.

Colors vary a bit from one Amish group to another, but, in general, the palette of Amish clothing leans toward only one-half of the full color wheel. The most dominant colors are the range from red-violet to, and including, green. These colors appear in various hues. The brighter, bolder purples, blues, pinks, and greens are likely to be used in dresses and shirts for young children while the darker, more subdued shades are worn by adults.

Nine-Patch, c. 1930–40. Cotton, 38 × 44. Holmes Co., Ohio. Collection of Catherine H. Anthony. A typical Amish pattern in typical Amish colors. The black squares create an additional chain pattern on the quilt surface.

Although simple in design and identical in pattern, little girls' dresses are of bright, cheerful colors. Many of these bold hues find their way into Amish quilts.

Bright reds, oranges and yellows, although avoided for outer clothing, were sometimes used as linings, facings, hems, and underdresses. Scraps from clothing construction were often utilized in quilt-making and these bright warm colors do appear in some quilts. Although reds, oranges, and yellows seldom appear in quilts of Lancaster County, Pennsylvania, Amish origin, they were frequently used in midwestern Amish quilts and in quilts from Amish groups in Mifflin County, Pennsylvania. Many Amish quilts also include touches of black. When used in cooperation with other vivid colors, black acts as a highlight and serves to brighten and intensify the whole. Neutral shades of brown and gray are also common.

Amish women had an uninhibited sense of color. They did not need to worry about color co-ordinating their own or their family's wardrobes, since that was already decided by the rules of the church. And since their homes were sparsely decorated (most have pale blue or green painted walls and no carpeting or draperies) they did not need to plan color schemes for their houses. This lack of color consciousness left them free to approach the color choices of a quilt top without the "rules" much of general society accepts. They were limited only by the quantity of their scrap bag and imaginations. And the local dry goods store could satisfy their imagination if their scrap bag could not.

In many quilts, the variety of fabrics used and the abundance of piecing done, even in small patches, would indicate that women often improvised with what they had rather than buying new fabric. They arranged their rainbow of colors in a way that seemed right to them. Even without a conscious understanding of what they were doing, many women constructed pieces using basic principles of color theory. Their unschooled eyes combined colors that brought out the best in each other. Many times the result was a blending of colors that only a secure or daring designer would attempt today.

Bear Paw, 1910. Cotton. 34 × 44. Iowa. Pat and Kemp Beall. Strong fabric contrasts define the pattern in clear sharp lines. Although the lines of the patches are jagged. when viewed as a whole the quilt has a soft. feathery effect.

Although many quilters did utilize fabrics from their scrap bags, it would be false to say that they made wholly scrap quilts. Large sections of fabric were required for borders and backings. Most women probably bought these pieces solely for quiltmaking. Since crib quilts obviously required less fabric than full-size quilts it is likely more of them were scrap quilts. Yet their finished appearance in many cases is evidence of pre-planned and thoughtful construction which may have required the purchase of specific fabrics. Other examples show piecing of even very tiny patches indicating that the quiltmaker was determined to make a quilt with what she had on hand.

Careful Workmanship

Making quilts and clothing for the family was a responsibility assumed by the woman of the house. Sometimes it was an enjoyed task and sometimes it was simply part of her job requirement. It is fair to assume that *some* of these so-called masterpieces were made not as a creative outlet, but out of sheer necessity to ward off the chill of winter nights. The principles of hard work and frugality were impetus enough to do any job to the best of one's ability. And the results were sometimes striking in both artistry and workmanship.

Amish quilts stand apart for their unusual attention to detail and quality workmanship. Antique Amish crib quilts are no exception. These small treasures were sewn and quilted with the same zeal for good workmanship.

Many Crib Quilts Worn to Shreds

Most Amish women did not make a lot of preparation before the birth of a new baby. In the early 20th century, infant mortality remained high. Pregnancy was a very private matter. In many cases women shared their secret only with their husbands and did not allow themselves to be seen in public. Although it was often a joyous condition, uncertainties made advance preparations less common than today. It was considered better to wait and see that everything would be without complications before collecting clothing and layette accessories. Thus crib quilts were made by mothers, grandmothers, aunts or other relatives after the baby arrived.

The average size of an Amish family was, and continues to be, seven children. This meant that children were often quite close in age. Obviously a mother did not have the time to make a quilt for each child. Also, it was not necessary. A house may have had one or two cribs, while it probably had four to six double-size beds. The quilt made for a first child could be handed down to younger siblings. And since fewer crib quilts were made, those that were used were worn to rags. Repeated usage and repeated washings destroyed many.

However, some of these treasures have been passed through the years and remain in remarkably good condition. These were likely either "Sunday quilts" or quilts that were put away as a memoir for a child. In the same way that some exceptional full-size quilts were used only on special occasions, some crib quilts were used similarly. Church held in the home would constitute a special occasion. One's best quilts would be displayed on the beds, making a lovely presentation for anyone who had reason to wander upstairs. The crib, in some cases, had its own quilt.

The types of fabrics used in crib quilts were most often cottons or, in some cases, fine wools. These natural fibers created a warm yet lightweight bedcover.

Crib Quilts—A Display of Affection

Why would these women, whose lives were so filled with families, gardens, and managing households, go to the effort to produce such striking bedcovers? The Amish are a people who believe and practice ideals of frugality and simplicity. Yet within the limitations they've chosen is space for individual expression and beauty. Quilts come under this category.

A quilt is a functional item and therefore not frivolous or unnecessary. The fact that

Children of Amish parents grow up eating, drinking, sleeping, and playing "Amishness." Theirs is a world that, like nested mixing bowls and concentric circles, mirrors their parents'.

these quilts go far beyond sheer necessity in their design and quilting does not pose a problem for the Amish. It is an area where a woman may demonstrate her skill as a seamstress and her ability as an artist. Although the Amish would not articulate it as such, quiltmaking seems to have been, and continues to be, an acceptable avenue for the flow of creativity. Quilts also stand as tangible statements of love and affection. Not only are these small quilts aesthetically pleasing, part of their charm is the underlying knowledge of the tenderness and love inherent in each tiny stitch. Children are loved and wanted in Amish culture and these quilts embody some of that feeling.

Quiltings Support Community Life

In a subculture that sets what appears to be severe restrictions on fun and leisure, Amish women find creative outlet in their work. Quilting was not only work, it was, and continues to be, a time to socialize and visit with friends around the quilting frame. The perimeters of a crib quilt stretched in a frame could only accommodate three or four quilters at a time. Therefore, these small quilts were often quilted by a single individual or family. So if one held a "quilting" for crib quilts it made sense to have two or more ready to be quilted, to make efficient use of the available hands. A quilting could be called at any time but was more likely to be held during seasons when garden work did not compete for time. It was often a whole day affair with the hostess serving a bountiful lunch for all who came to help. Around the quilt, women shared thoughts and ideas, gained from each other support and reassurance in their roles as wives and mothers, and got a break from the routine of daily life.

Who Are the Amish?

The Amish are a Christian group who trace their religious roots to the radical wing of the Protestant Reformation in 16th

Sunshine and Shadow. c. 1930. Cotton. rayon. 46 × 46. Intercourse. Pennsylvania. Dr. and Mrs. Donald M. Herr. The pattern. wide borders. and corner blocks make this a typical Lancaster County Amish quilt. A lovely trailing rose quilting motif adorns the border.

No one on an Amish farm punches a time clock. Days are long. Work is hard. Everyone helps. But there is joy and contentment in learning to live and love and work together.

century Europe. This group was eventually nicknamed Anabaptists because they rebaptised adults. Several characteristics of Anabaptists are 1) their acceptance of the Bible as a normative guide for life; 2) adult, voluntary baptism; 3) separation of church and state; 4) the practice of peace and non-resistance in all facets of life.

The Amish believe God has called them to a life of faithfulness. They feel they can best live their convictions by drawing lines between themselves and the world. Ways in which the Amish separate themselves can appear comic if any single practice is highlighted outside of its context. But seen as a whole, Amish society offers its members a viable and happy way of life. Most Amish drive horses and buggies instead of cars. Their dress is simple and basic. Their intent is modesty; they simply ignore the competition of fashion. Distinctive language also helps keep the Amish people together, and separate from the world. With the completion of grade eight, most Amish children end their formal education.

This community is severely skeptical of high technology and electronics. Consequently, alternative energy sources are the norm for the Amish since they do not use electricity from public utilities. The gradual, unconscious assimilation of their people into the larger society is a fear of Amish leaders. The drawing of stark lines provides a visible distinction between the Amish and the world around them.

A Word About This Book's Organization

This book is structured around the seasons of a child's life. The quilts in each section might easily fit into any season, however.

The introductions to the seasonal sections are fictional creations of the authors, inspired by many stories heard in person or read in Amish periodicals. The stories and poetry elsewhere were selected from Amish publications as credited.

Grandmother's Flower Garden, c. 1920. Cotton. 31 × 45. Ohio. Judi Boisson Antique American Quilts, New York City, Southampton. Light, soft colors create a quiet, tranquil quilt. Hexagon shapes are joined together to form flowers. Flowers are separated with a blue path.

Spring

Spring

Mama's all excited. Daddy hitched up the team and worked up the garden. Now we can plant peas. We're doing five long rows this year. At planting it seems Mama always forgets how long those rows get when picking time comes.

I'll help plant again this year. Mama goes from row to row checking to make sure we've dropped them just the right space apart. The fun part is covering them. The dirt is mounded up in little ridges along both sides of the furrow where the plow went. I like to kick those ridges down real gently over the peas. They need to be covered just deep enough for protection from the cool nights but not so deep that the tender sprouts can't push through.

All the time we plant I think ahead to the first picking when Mama will gather a mess of the first tender peas and make a big steaming dish of pea pot pie for supper. The tiny new peas play hide and seek under the big doughy pot pie squares floating in cream with melted butter. It's one of Daddy's favorite suppers.

I keep watching for bumble bees. Mama always says it's not warm enough to go barefoot until the locust trees bloom and the bumble bees are out. She means those great big bees that buzz real slowly through the air and suddenly dart up or down. Sometimes the boys and I whack at them with a piece of tobacco lath and try to knock them down in midair.

School will soon be out for the summer. The last day is our picnic. We'll have a program in the morning and then lunch and games. We've learned some new songs and I'm saying a poem that I wrote about daffodils. It's kinda scary to stand up in front of all the parents and other brothers and sisters, but it's always a real special day. Everyone brings food to share for lunch. Mama makes good packed lunches but nothing can beat that whole table full of casseroles, pies, cakes, and salads where you can choose whatever you want.

Last night when I went to the cellar to get potatoes for supper I noticed the bin was nearly empty. Mama had gone through and picked out some of the smaller potatoes to use for seed. They're in the cellar in a tomato basket. They look funny—all wrinkled with long whitish sprouts peeking out between the basket slats.

Soon after peas we'll plant potatoes. Mama and I will sit out on the back porch and cut the potatoes in quarters, making sure each section has an eye so the potato can sprout. Some people make sure that eye is looking up when they drop the potato in the row to help it sprout more easily. We never pay attention to that. We just plop ours in the row however they fall. They always come up fine for us.

We dig our first new potatoes to eat with new peas. Then they're still small. I like the tiny marble-sized ones swimming in browned butter. When they're new we just scrub them and eat them, skin and all. We do that until they've been stored for a while. Then the skin gets tough and kinda bitter. I get so tired of peeling all those potatoes when their skins aren't good to eat any more.

We've begun spring housecleaning. We start upstairs and do one room at a time. Mama and Leah started yesterday while we were at school. When we came home they had the rag carpet from the hallway draped over the washline. The boys beat it and carried it back in. We wipe all the ceilings and walls with a damp cloth.

I usually don't like washing windows except in ours and the boys' bedrooms at the front of the house. The porch roof is right outside those windows. Mama sends Sara out on the roof and I do the inside while Sara does the outside. I'd like to go out too but Mama thinks the two of us would get silly and she's afraid we'd fall off. We only do the second floor windows at houseclean-

Family ties are close. Parents and children interact frequently in work and play. Children learn responsibility early in life and are involved in daily chores.

ing time. The first floor is easier to get at and Mama insists that they stay sparkling clear.

When we took the mattress from our room to air it out Sara and I found a dress for our doll Molly that had been lost for weeks. Somehow it had slipped down between the foot board and the mattress and must have gotten tucked in under with a sheet. Anyway, there it was, all pressed flat under the weight of the mattress. Sara laughed and said maybe Molly has grown too much and it won't fit her anymore. The rooms smell so good after housecleaning. Seems like we bring spring right into the house.

Crocuses are blooming along the porch where they're protected. Before long we'll be able to dig up the flower beds and plant pansies. Groossmammi likes pansies. She says they have such pretty little faces.

Fluffy had twin lambs. They're jumping all around the meadow. They don't like to be petted yet but we'll get them tame. Jonas was trying to catch one and ran smack into a groundhog hole and twisted his ankle

pretty bad. That lamb sure got the best of him.

I took some soup over to the other end of the house to give to Daadi and Groossmammi for supper. Groossmammi still cooks but Mama and Daddy worry about her burning herself so Mama sends hot food over once each day. Groossmammi was cutting quilt patches. Mama gives her the scraps left over from our dresses and the boys' shirts. She's cutting squares for a Sunshine and Shadow quilt. She marks each one individually. She needs cutting lines for each patch because her hands shake. She's always been a real fussy quilt-maker and she wants the pieces to be exactly square. Sometimes I stay and eat with her and Daadi. We visit and tell stories while we do dishes.

One of our best cows is down. Daddy went up to the neighbors to call the vet. When he got here he looked her over real good and gave her a shot. He thinks she'll pull through fine. Daddy and Mama are sure relieved. She's one of our best cows and milk prices are high now.

Stars. c. 1885. Cotton. 34 × 40. Holmes Co.. Ohio. Sandra Mitchell. *Half of these stars seem to signal the arrival of day and the other half the onset of night. Although the quilting lines are simple straight lines. their precision and abundance make an attractive pattern.*

Hole in the Barn Door, c. 1910–20. Cotton, 33 × 41. LaGrange Co., Indiana. Rebecca Haarer. Solid pink blocks alternated with the pieced ones allow space for a large floral quilting design. A bright red binding adds spark.

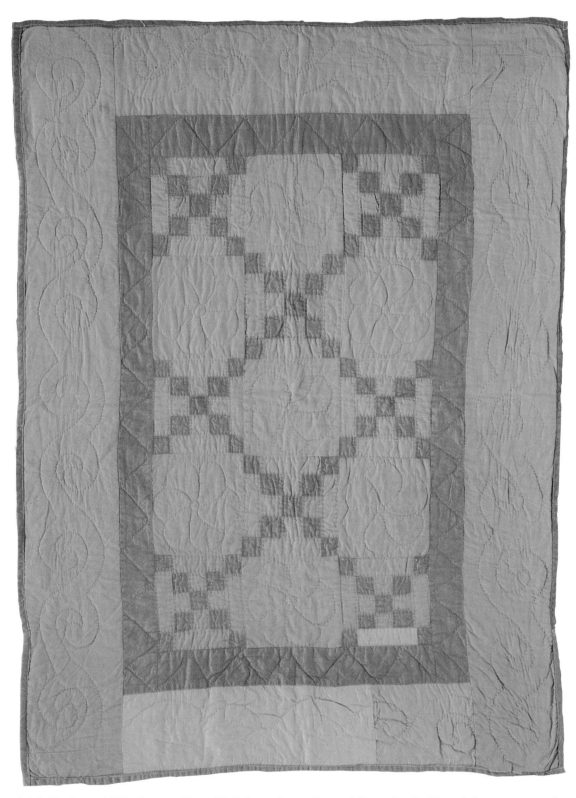

Irish Chain, c. 1930. Cotton, 28 × 37. Kalona, Iowa. Pat and Kemp Beall. Tiny pink squares track a chain over the turquoise background. Note the fabric change on the one border width. The matches were close but not identical.

Lead Us Not Into Temptation

When I was a girl we lived on a farm in a long lane. Standing in our barnyard was a tall windmill which pumped water for the livestock. Sometimes when the fire whistle sounded in town, our father would climb up the windmill to look if he could see any smoke.

One Sunday my parents were invited to a relative for dinner. Because my three-year-old brother had pinkeye we couldn't all go along. So Mother left two of us girls at home with him. Since I was the oldest in the family, Mother warned me to keep an eye on him, but to let him play outside in the afternoon, as it was such a nice day.

We did as we were told and that afternoon when I looked out the window he was busy playing in the barnyard. I went back to my reading. How long I read, I do not know (it might have been longer than I thought), it seemed like only a short time until I looked out the window again. Where was my little brother? The toys he had been playing with were in the barnyard but no little boy was to be seen. Quickly I went outside and called his name.

Soon I heard him answer but at first I couldn't tell from which direction his voice had come. Then I looked up and saw him. He had only three more steps to go to be at the top of the 50-ft. windmill. Fear instantly gripped me. What could I do?

I knew that going to the neighbors for help would not be a good idea, for he could fall down a long time before I returned. I was afraid to go up since we children had always been forbidden by our parents to climb the windmill. Even if I could get the courage to climb up to him, how would I ever be able to get us both down? So I decided to do the only thing I knew to do.

I talked to him calmly and pretended I was not alarmed that he was up there. I could see the little fellow wasn't afraid so I told him to climb back down again. Calmly and slowly he started downward, holding tightly to the iron rung with his chubby little hands. About half ways down he almost missed a step. I held my breath, but he wasn't scared. "Oops!" he said and tried again. Slowly he kept coming until he was safely down.

(Family Life)

New life seems to be everywhere around an Amish farmstead. But despite its frequency, curiosity, fun and birth seem to go hand in hand.

Fence Row variation, c. 1910. Cotton, 34 × 44. Ohio. Judi Boisson Antique American Quilts, New York City, Southampton. Even when utilizing fabric scraps, the quilter seems to have had an overall plan. Note the symmetrical piecing on the lengths of the inner border.

Nine-Patch in Diamond, 1930. Cotton. 40 × 58. Lawrence Co., Pennsylvania. Private collection. Assorted Nine-Patch blocks are set against pieced blocks of bright pink and turquoise. The overall effect is certainly stimulating.

Triangles, c. 1940. Cotton, 30 × 40. Holmes Co., Ohio. Collection of Eve and David Wheatcroft, Lewisburg, PA. Carefully arranged triangles create a sailboat effect. All is restrained within the dark border.

Humility is an important virtue. A prescribed style of dress encourages the spirit of community rather than individual pride.

After making a new organdy covering for one of the little girls, I had it lying on the ironing board all ironed nicely and ready to wear. She admired it awhile then asked if she could try it on. So I put it on her. She gently ran her hand along the back, then asked, "Mom, does it look like a cake from the back?" In her eyes a neatly rounded covering made her think of cake. I could tell she was proud of such a covering. Burning with shame on the inside, I wondered why I had spent so much time in making it so nice and round if that was sowing seeds of pride in her heart. Where can we draw the line between neatness and pride?

—*A Learning Mother*
(Family Life)

Our five-year-old was explaining to her brother that neighbor Jakes got a baby boy because they needed a boy to help them with the chores. Her little brother wisely told her that they didn't choose a boy. They were given a boy and you don't refuse what someone gives you and say you want something else. In his innocence he was right because we all know we can't choose between a boy or girl. In other things too we can't choose our blessings. We should accept what the Lord sees fit to bless us with, instead of murmuring and asking for something different.

—*A mother*
(Family Life)

Nine-Patch in Blockwork, c. 1930. Cotton. 43 × 63. Mifflin Co., Pennsylvania. Daniel J. and Kathryn M. McCauley. Geometric piecework is surrounded by delicately quilted tulips and framed in a border of quilted cable.

Log Cabin—Barnraising variation. c. 1920. Cotton sateens and wool. 34 × 34. LaGrange Co., Indiana. Faye and Don Walters. Colors seem to be mixed randomly throughout this quilt but the maker has achieved the barnraising design with the consistent use of black.

Sunshine and Shadow in a Diamond. c. 1900. Wool and cotton. 44 × 44. Lancaster Co., Pennsylvania. Dr. and Mrs. Donald M. Herr. Beautiful feather quilting fills the outer border of this quilt. Generous quilting spills over to the inner border as well. The pieced design is enhanced with straight line quilting.

Variable Star variation. 1920. Cotton. 42 × 57. Mifflin Co., Pennsylvania. Private collection. Skill-ful use of light, medium, and darker fabric hues give the pieced stars dimension. Beautiful maple leaves are quilted on the inner border.

Children emulate their parents in appearance and function. Little girls learn by helping and will one day be able to perform the tasks of their mothers. Thus, a sense of being Amish is passed from generation to generation.

My Later Days

When I grow up, I'd like to be,
A housewife working cheerily,
Tasks in summer I would do,
Are picking strawberries that grew.
And crawling down upon my knees,
I'd search for carrots, beans and peas.
I'd also have to mow the lawn,
And water plants at break of dawn.

And as the summer wore away,
Housecleaning time would come to stay;

I'd clean the rooms one by one,
And think the work was lots of fun.
And then to settle down to sew,
Some clothes before we see it snow;
I'd sometimes have a quilting bee,
And ask my friends to come to me.

Now this is what I'd like to be,
When I grow up, as you can see.
And now what I would like to hear,
Is what you choose for your career.
—Grade 7
(Blackboard Bulletin)

Togetherness is a part of being Amish. Without cars, telephones or electricity they spend more time at home with each other than do most other Americans.

Rainy Days

On rainy days we like to play
At Grandpa's house not far away,
We hop into our black raincoats
And walk along the muddy roads.
Until we reach the house so tall
And hear our Grandma's welcome call,
For us to stay half of the day
And then we should be on our way.

The attic is our favorite spot
It's not too cold and not too hot,
For us to play hide-and-go-seek
Upon the olden floors which creak.

And when we're tired of it all
We step out in the great big hall,
And then we play some games out there
Till Grandma comes up on the stair.

Cookies and lemonade she brings
Plus a dozen of other things,
Grandpa is right behind her too
Bringing with him a good hot stew.
Then it is time to say "Good Bye,"
Which makes my sister almost cry.
Until one more rainy day will come
Again we'll over to Grandpa's run.

—Grade 8, Age 13, Ontario
(Blackboard Bulletin)

Bars-Roman Coin variation, c. 1920. Cotton and wool, 41 × 47. Indiana. Judi Boisson Antique Amish Quilts, New York City, Southampton. This pattern could utilize many small snippets of fabric. One piece of printed fabric sneaked into the center bar.

Old Maid's Puzzle, 1927. Cotton, 48 × 59. Kalona, Iowa. Pat and Kemp Beall. Blue triangles seem to float in the salmon colored blocks. A well planned and well executed quilt.

Summer

Summer

There was a ferocious thunderstorm last night. At the supper table, Daddy fussed about how hot and sticky it felt and said he was sure there'd be a storm before midnight. It seems thunderstorms always are worse after dark and this one hit just after I'd fallen asleep. Sometimes I wish I didn't have to share a bedroom with anyone but last night I was mighty glad to have Sara there in bed beside me. We pulled the sheet up over our heads when the lightning flashed. Mama came in to make sure all the windows were closed so it wouldn't rain in. This morning the corn, especially in the south field, was bent way over but Daddy says it will stand up again.

The strawberries are about over. We picked five quarts this morning but they're small and sorta knotty. Mama crushed them and later this afternoon we're making homemade strawberry ice cream. Mama sent Levi across the fields to ask Lydia and the children to come join us. John got sick and died last year and Lydia has to work real hard to keep the farm. Mama and Daddy sorta look out for her. Daddy and our boys help out during the busiest field work, but Daddy always says after he comes home how responsible John's boys are. Daddy always liked John and he misses him when our families are together.

Lydia's girls go to market. After John died, the man they work for offered some space on his stand if Lydia wanted to do baking to help with some income. Now each week they make homemade potato rolls and sell them along with the bologna, cheeses, and other sandwich meats the stand always had. They have some real regular customers who say no one makes better rolls than Lydia. I hope Lydia gets married again someday but it's hard to imagine she'd find anyone as nice as John. They seemed real happy together.

We got a letter from Ben and Elizabeth. They moved north to where land was a little cheaper and set up housekeeping there.

Elizabeth is real busy since the twins were born, but she said she has good help from the neighbors and the babies are pleasant. Ben's sister had twins, too, so she knows how it is.

Daddy saw an ad in the newspaper that cherries will be in next week. We'll take a bunch of buckets and go by bus to pick cherries to can. The bus connections are good and we only have to walk a little piece from where it drops us to where we pick. We pick about equal amounts of sour cherries and the big dark sweet cherries. Mama always picks some of the big light sweet ones too, 'cause she likes those in fruit salad.

It's more fun to pick the sweet ones 'cause you can eat while you pick. The orchard charges per pound of cherries. Daddy always says he thinks they should weigh us along with the buckets of cherries because we've eaten so many.

Picking is fun, but sitting around taking out all those seeds isn't. Daddy and Mama always say that many hands make light work so even the boys help seed cherries. We all sit around in the washhouse and dig the seeds out with the rounded end of a hairpin. Even if you're real careful the juice squirts and gets all over the place. That's why we use the washhouse. When we're done we just rinse things down with the hose and sweep the water down the drain. We tried doing it outside once but the flies were too pesty.

We can the sweet cherries with the seeds in them and then spit them out as we eat them. Packing the cherries in the jars goes quickly and we can have them picked, jarred and sealed all in one day. That means a lot of cherries, cherry pies, and cherry cobbler for the winter. A few hours of sticky seeding are worth that.

We have early corn on our roadside stand. City people drive out of their way to buy corn from us. Our corn is fresh-picked every day. We go through half the patch in

The Amish care for both their young and their old. Houses can sprout several add-ons, providing private quarters for parents and grandparents. Three generations are common, with responsibilities and care being shared by all.

the morning before breakfast and then pick more during the day as it's needed. Mama opens each ear before she puts it on the stand to make sure it's filled out nice and there are no worms. We plant corn at different times so we have different patches getting ready all through the summer. We sell the first pickings on the roadside stand since those ears are the nicest.

Towards the end the ears aren't as nice. We call those the "nubbins." They taste just as good. We freeze those. We don't have a freezer at our house so we haul it to the frozen food locker about two miles up the road. We rent space there and just take home what will fit in the freezer compartment above our refrigerator. The locker is real handy for us. Some people we know in the next county can't get to a locker. They share some space in a freezer with their non-Amish neighbors.

Levi brought in a baby bunny he found along the edge of the field when he was cutting alfalfa. He said the horses stepped right over the nest. Mama said he's cute now but he'd better not nibble her garden. We took him back out to the field and left him go.

It keeps us stepping to have enough cookies on hand these days. We baked three batches just this week. Taking lemonade and cookies out to the fields makes them go fast. I help stack bales for a while after the lemonade break so I can ride a full wagon back in to the house. I like the ride. Helping to unload isn't much fun, though. It makes me itchy just to think about it.

Groossmammi's quilt is nearly all pieced. She's only been able to work a little at a time. The stiffness in her knees makes it hard to treadle the machine. The quilt top looks real nice. Groossmammi's not so good but she never complains. She says she's just thankful her mind is still clear. At 89 her memory is as sharp as mine. She thinks it can't be that she forgot to send cousin Joe's Mary a birthday card until the day before. That's better than me. I would have forgotten it altogether.

Grandmother's Flower Garden, c. 1920. Cotton, 32 × 33. LaGrange Co., Indiana. Rebecca Haarer. This flower grows in expanding rings from one central hexagon. The quilt is brightened and highlighted by its red border.

Chimney Sweep, c. 1915. Cotton. 35 × 36. Ohio. Scott and Cindy Albright. Delicate in both pieced pattern and quilting designs, this quilt provided a challenge for its maker. The reverse side is solid black with a red inner border.

Bow Tie, c. 1900. Wool, 33 × 40. LaGrange Co., Indiana. Rebecca Haarer. Dark bow ties are cleverly disguised among bright octagons. The shade of the dark fabric varies slightly throughout the quilt.

I Wanted the Biggest Piece

Years ago when I was a little girl of around nine years old, my mother used to send me to the local grocery store. I was hardly ever allowed to buy candy, but on one rare occasion she gave me a penny to buy a piece of gum. I knew exactly which kind I wanted—the little pink rectangular piece that looked like an eraser.

However, when I got to the store, they also had another kind that I hadn't ever seen before. It was flat and wrapped up like a piece of regular chewing gum. I stood there for a long time, trying to decide which piece was the biggest one. Finally I picked up the one I had originally planned on buying, because it was thicker.

Then I went to get the rest of the things Mother had on the list, but my mind was still turning over the question of whether or not I had made the right choice.

After having paid for everything else, I headed for the door. On the way out I had to pass the candy shelf again. There were those tempting pieces of gum. And sure enough, by now the other kind looked much bigger than the one I had bought! No one was watching, so I quickly exchanged the one I had bought for the other one, telling myself that there wasn't anything wrong with it. I had, after all, paid for a piece of gum, and they were both the same price.

But for some reason, I felt guilty about what I was doing. As I turned to leave, I looked back and saw the owner of the store looking at me from around the corner. Quickly I ducked out the door, hoping he had not seen what I had done. Later I often wished I had faced him and explained what I had done. As it was, I was sure he thought I had stolen the piece of gum, and for a long time afterwards, I always had the feeling he was watching me closely when I was in the store.

To add to my unhappiness, when I put the gum into my mouth, I discovered that it wasn't nearly as good as the kind I was well familiar with. That was one time when my greed brought me much unhappiness.

—Older and Wiser Now.
Pennsylvania
(Family Life)

Simple pleasures are the best. What could be more satisfying than a cone filled with cold, smooth ice cream dipped from a freezer you just helped turn?

Unnamed Pattern, c. 1930–35. Cotton, 38 × 55. Pennsylvania. Collection of Barbara S. Janow and Barbara Ross. Clever use of color makes this simple pattern of squares and triangles appear very complex. A unique and unusual adventure in quiltmaking.

Ocean Waves, 1919. Cotton, 33 × 37. Wayne Co., Ohio. Scott and Cindy Albright. The simple contrast of two fabrics makes this a striking and dynamic quilt.

Lemoyne Star, c. 1900. Cotton, 37 × 37. Homes Co., Ohio. Collection of Eve and David Wheatcroft, Lewisburg, PA. The lighter pink fabric in combination with more intense colors creates the illusion of movement in the stars.

After chores there is time to enjoy the long summer days. The catch may be slim, but relaxation and fun are adequate rewards.

H-m-m-m, Turtle Soup!

One day when Mother was hanging out the wash she heard the cows mooing and saw they were watching something. She went over to the field and saw a big snapping turtle. She called Dad and us children to come and look.

The turtle was very cross and snappy. Dad picked him up by his shell, but he tried to get away. He reached up with his big claws and scratched Dad's hands. He also pushed his tail hard against Dad and tried to turn around and bite him. When we finally got the turtle home and weighed him we discovered that he weighed thirty pounds!

Some men were building a barn at my uncle's place, so father took our turtle over there. They teased him with a stick until he got very cross and stuck out his head to grab the stick. Then they shot him in the head.

That evening Dad took him to some neighbor's place to learn how to butcher him. Then we invited some neighbors in for turtle soup and ice cream. We had a lot of fun playing games and telling the turtle story.

—Grade 7, Age 12, Pennsylvania
(Blackboard Bulletin)

Lone Star, 1937. Cotton, 39 × 49. Thomas, Oklahoma. Pat and Kemp Beall. The dark red in the star against a dark red field appears to separate the outer points from the center. The star seems to burst with energy.

Variable Star, c. 1910. Cotton, 37 × 43. Sugarcreek, Ohio. Scott and Cindy Albright. Unusual nine-patch corner blocks and a triple inner border frame the twinkling stars.

*Variable Star, c. 1890. Cotton, 26 × 35. Adams Co., Indiana. Daniel J. and Kathryn M. McCauley.
Sawtooth borders are never easy. This quilter had a different solution for each corner.*

Four-Patch variation, c. 1910–20. 34 × 37. Holmes Co., Ohio. Collection of Eve and David Wheatcroft, Lewisburg, PA. Four-patch blocks in a multitude of colors surround black crosses which are consistent throughout. All is contained inside yellow and red borders.

Everything is better when shared with a friend. In Amish society, joys are multiplied and sorrows are lessened by the support of a loving, caring community.

An Unusual Surprise

One rainy Sunday when we came home from church we invited Grandpas over for supper. They live right next door to us. After supper Grandpa and us children wanted to go back to where the church had been, as they had a singing. But Grandma, Dad and Mom didn't want to go, so Grandma said that if Grandpa would wash the dishes we would all go with him. So, to our surprise, he jumped right up and started clearing the table. After clearing the table he began washing the dishes, but I don't know how clean he got them! My 6-year-old brother of course pitied him, and started rinsing the dishes for him.

While they were washing dishes the rest of us got ready to go.

Suddenly I had an idea. I got one of Mom's brown aprons and tied it around his waist. How we laughed, for he looked so funny!

So we found a new way to get the dishes washed, but I don't know how often it will work!

—*Grade 6, Age 12*
(Blackboard Bulletin)

Big animals and little children are standard fare around the farm. Mutual respect is learned early. Mutual dependence continues throughout life for the Amish since animals help provide livelihood, transportation and energy sources for the people.

When I Grow Up

When I grow up I would like to have a good wife, some children to trail behind me, and enough land to build a house, a barn, and a hog building on it. I would like to be an auctioneer to sell things at a farm sale because they help people get rid of things they don't want anymore by selling them and getting a good price for the things.

In my spare time I would like to do some carpenter work, which is what my father does.

Even if I wish I could do those things, I will just take what comes.

—Grade 7, Age 13
(Blackboard Bulletin)

When I Grow Up

When I grow up I would like to be a farmer, especially in summer, when it is so warm. I would like to have about fifteen cows and have children trailing behind me to help. In my spare time I would like to travel or fish.

In winter I would like to farm some of the time and not milk so many cows. In my spare time I would love to hunt. I probably would have to shovel snow in winter, too, or make snowmen for the little children. We'd be a happy and content family, enjoying many pleasant times together.

—Grade 5, Age 11, Indiana
(Blackboard Bulletin)

Roman Coin variation, c. 1920–25. Cotton, 39 × 48. Mifflin Co., Pennsylvania. Private collection. Strips of various widths are pieced together to form squares. Set between these squares are solid blocks of fabric quilted with a double heart motif.

Nine-Patch, c. 1920. Cotton and cotton sateen, 32 × 43. Holmes Co., Ohio. Collection of Eve and David Wheatcroft, Lewisburg, PA. This quilt uses a variety of fabrics in an almost random fashion, but the consistent use of black unifies the whole.

Fall

Fall

I don't know if I ever heard a pig squeal louder. Jonas said he thinks it's because the pig thought he was safe since he had sorta been Jonas's pet. But I guess that's the price you pay for being friends with something you know will be butchered some day. I wonder if Jonas will be able to enjoy the bacon later on in the winter. I never watch the butchering until I know the pig is dead and they start scraping it.

We were right about Eli Esh's down the road. All the celery they had trenched did show up on Naomi and Christ's wedding table. Mama often says, watch the celery patches to know who's getting married in November. Daddy and Mama have nine weddings this season. One every single Tuesday and Thursday in November and one the first Tuesday of December. It's always sorta fun when I get to go—especially the afternoons. I get so tired of sitting the whole morning in the service sometimes I think my seat's going to be flat forever. After lunch we sit around and tell stories. I love it. And in the evenings there's often singing.

We have a new teacher this year. She used to teach over at Morris Run School. Since our teacher last year plans to get married this fall she said she didn't want to teach anymore. So we got the Morris Run teacher and they got one of last year's eighth grade girls to teach. I think Teacher will be nice except she's so picky about keeping our lunch boxes on the shelf right above our coat hooks. Everybody knows what their own lunch box looks like anyhow. I don't see why it matters.

Mama promised we could go to Miller's on Saturday and get some cloth to make me a new Sunday dress. She said mine's showing so much wear that it should be for everyday instead of for good. I always get a kick out of going to Miller's. They sell all kinds of little doodle pads with games and puzzles. Last time we went Mama said I didn't need another one already. But now I've done all the puzzles and I'm pretty sure she'll let me get another one again. I hope so, anyhow.

I think we finally mowed the lawn for the last time. Daddy said he thinks it's done till spring. We'll probably still have to rake the leaves one more time. There are still some hanging up high.

Groossmammi brought the quilting templates back this morning. Said she has it all marked and ready to put in. She asked Mama if she'd help stretch it in the frame this afternoon. They'll set it right inside the window so she can see better to quilt when the sun is high. I get a funny feeling all over when I see her trying to get around. It goes so hard for her. Mama says she can't imagine she'll be with us much longer. But she's so spunky. Even though she's pretty weak she sure likes to quilt. No one close to us ever died before. I don't want to think about it.

Ben and Leah are going to Melinda's sing-

The Amish usually own and operate their own schools. They place a high value on wisdom which they believe can best be learned through practical experience within their own community.

ing this weekend. Ben says he guesses they'll sweep off the big barn floor and have it there. In about five or six years I should be able to go along.

Amos King's had sale last week. There were tons of people there. And the prices people paid for some of the stuff was crazy. Daddy said he'd be happy to save some of his socks until they got to be old antiques and would sell for $80.00 apiece. An old quilt went through the roof. I didn't understand exactly how much it brought. Leah said she thought over $2,000.00. Woweezowee! I wish I had a couple of them lying around.

I helped for awhile at the food stand. They said I could have up to $3.00 worth of free food for helping. I had chicken corn soup, barbeque and an apple dumpling. That wasn't quite $3.00 worth, but I was full, so I put what was left in the donation box. All the money they collected was going to help with the hospital expenses

from when Steve Lapp got his foot in the corn chopper and had to have an operation.

Daddy and the boys think they'll get the corn all shocked next week. That's always a happy time. That wraps up most of the field work for another year.

Maple Leaf, c. 1920. Cotton and cotton sateens, 33 × 37. Holmes Co., Ohio. Collection of Eve and David Wheatcroft, Lewisburg, PA. An unusual pattern for Amish quiltmakers. Blue leaves seem to flutter against the black field.

Stars, c. 1935. Cotton and cotton sateens, 35 × 41. Holmes Co., Ohio. Collection of Eve and David Wheatcroft, Lewisburg, PA. Good proportions and strong fabric contrasts make this a stunning little quilt.

Variable Star, c. 1885. Cotton. 33 × 34. Holmes Co., Ohio. Sandra Mitchell. This is clearly the work of a skilled quilter. Little space was left unstitched.

Our Project at School

We have an interesting project at our school. In the beginning of the term our teacher gave us each a notebook to use as a diary. Every evening we have ten minutes of free time to write the happenings of the day into our diary.

We don't have to worry about someone snooping in our desk and reading our diary, because the teacher promised she wouldn't and if any of the pupils do, we may think up a suitable punishment for them, such as having them read a whole page out of their diary out loud in front of the school, or sitting in their desks at recess.

This way we learn to respect other people's personal things and to leave things alone that aren't any of our business. If we forget what happened a certain day in school, we can easily check in our diary. In later years we can also look back and read about our school life, how we acted, and things like that. If we are ever teachers, I'm sure we will be able to get valuable tips out of our diaries by reading about the things our teacher did in school, which we may forget altogether if we don't write them down.

—Bloomfield, Iowa
(Blackboard Bulletin)

Free Time Project

We have a very interesting project going at our school which we all enjoy. Every week on Monday, our teacher credits us with twenty minutes of "free time." But it doesn't stay twenty minutes very long, because our teacher subtracts a minute for every piece of paper he has to pick up from the floor inside, or the playground outside. Also if we whisper during school hours when it isn't necessary, or disobey any of our other rules, he subtracts five minutes.

We may add minutes by all being in our seats by a minute and a half after the bell rings. Then on Friday we spend the number of minutes we have left playing softball or volleyball. We do not always have twenty minutes left, but if we don't, we know it is our own fault.

This project helps keep the schoolground clean, helps us remember to hurry to our seats when the bell rings, and also reminds us not to whisper. You can imagine why we think this is interesting. Best of all, it is fun!

—Grade 7, Indiana
(Blackboard Bulletin)

The basics of reading, writing and arithmetic are taught in Amish schools. Most Amish children do not go to school beyond the eighth grade. Although formal education is discontinued, practical experience is a lifelong teacher.

Log Cabin, c. 1900. Cotton and wool, 31 × 42. Holmes Co., Ohio. Collection of Eve and David Wheatcroft, Lewisburg, PA. The pieced border and sashing between the patches make this an unusual example of a Log Cabin quilt.

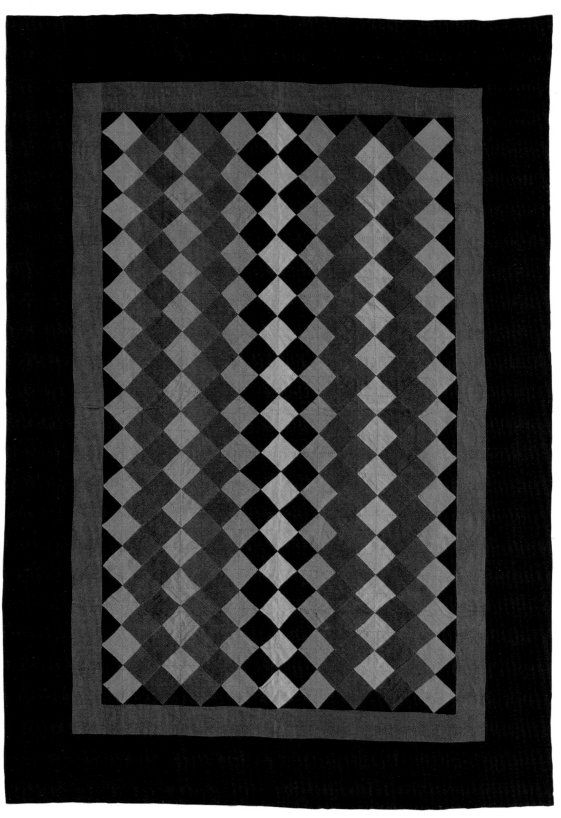

One-Patch, 1932. Wool, 46 × 64. Topeka, Indiana. Rebecca Haarer. This quilt must have rarely been used for it has been preserved in impeccable condition. The date is quilted in two corners.

Fence Row variation, c. 1890. Cotton. 47 × 75. Ohio. Judi Boisson Antique American Quilts. New York City. Southampton. A multitude of carefully pieced fabrics provide the background for lavish quilting designs.

There is joy at harvest. Keenly implanted in Amish consciousness is the axiom that one reaps what one sows. This belief is understood in the field and on the church bench alike.

Autumn

What is better than autumn days?
Outdoors the geese are calling.
Upon the farm and in the woods,
The golden leaves are falling.

Corn and potatoes and pumpkins;
The harvest in the fall
Makes lots of work from dawn to dusk,
From morn to supper call.

Autumn is cold and it is warm;
Autumn is windy and gay;
I have always thought that autumn
Is just as good as May.

Oh, what is better than autumn,
Than through the woods to rove?
When geese are calling overhead,
Who could stay beside the stove?
—Grade 8, Indiana

(Blackboard Bulletin)

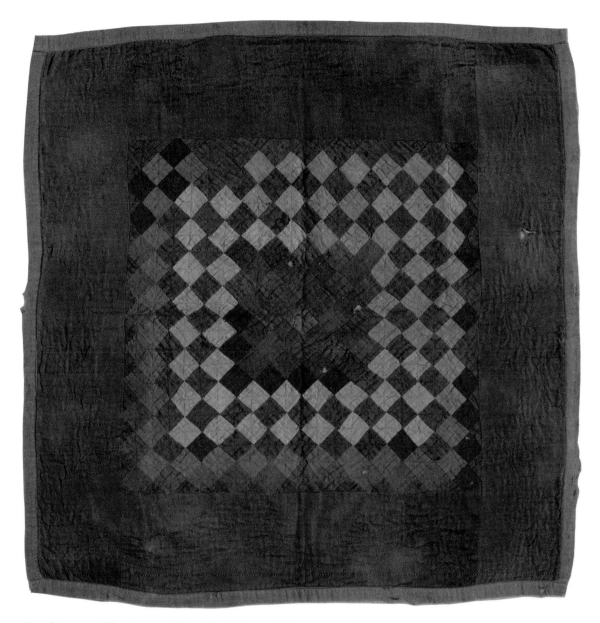

Sunshine and Shadow, c. 1890. Wool, 36 × 36. Lancaster Co., Pennsylvania. Collection of Eve and David Wheatcroft, Lewisburg, PA. Although badly worn, this quilt typifies Lancaster County Amish quilts in proportion, color, and workmanship.

Stairway to Heaven, c. 1900. Wool, 31 × 37. LaGrange Co., Indiana. Rebecca Haarer. An unusual variation of the Bars pattern.

Four-Patch, 1925. Cotton, rayon and cotton sateen, 34 × 40. Mifflin Co., Pennsylvania. Private collection. Cool blue and purple are warmed by the brown background in this simple but eloquent quilt.

Unnamed pattern, c. 1880. Wool, 50 × 56. LaGrange Co., Indiana. Collection of Barbara S. Janos and Barbara Ross. The large central design is flanked by a checkerboard inner border with small squares on the sides and larger ones on top and bottom. Sturdy tulips are quilted along top and bottom border and in corner squares.

Recess is a time for boisterous, wholesome fun. Children of different ages interact in play as well as in the classroom setting.

Rescuing the Ball

I would like to tell you about a strange happening we had this year. One day the lower graders were playing "Andy Over" over the schoolhouse. All at once the playing stopped and the children said the ball had gone down the chimney.

A few days later the boys brought a ladder and a big coon-hunting flashlight along to school. They climbed up and flashed into the chimney. They told us they could see the ball way down at the bottom. (The bottom of the chimney is in the basement.)

The chimney has an opening, but not all the way at the bottom. One day we decided to use a hose and see if we could float the ball to the opening where we could get it.

We pumped and pumped. One of the girls got a mirror and tried to look down the chimney where the ball was. When she reached in, the ball was right in front or her, so she reached in and got it.

The distance between the bottom of the chimney and the opening is around four feet, so you can know we pumped hundreds of strokes on our hand pump. But it was worth it, because we got our ball back. We used it to play "Rabbit" today.

—Grade 6, Age 12, Indiana
(Blackboard Bulletin)

The Amish are an industrious, hard-working people. Energies are harnessed and channeled in positive directions. Even the smallest bundles of energy are carefully tended.

When I Grow Up

When I grow up I want to be an old maid. I want to live in a small house all by myself. There would be a little woods just outside my house. I'd also have a small barn. I'd keep a horse, buggy, and harness, chickens, and a goat inside the barn. Then I wouldn't need to buy milk and eggs for myself. I'd have a little garden somewhere on my little place too. I'd plant plenty of vegetables. I wouldn't plant soybeans because I don't like to pick them. I'd be very particular to keep the weeds out of my garden.

I'd have a little shop. In there I'd bake hundreds of delicious loaves of bread. I'd add raisins to it and put frosting on top.

In my spare time I'd go out to the woods and watch the birds, knit booties to sell or give away, visit a friend, read a book, write to a friend, or anything else I'd be interested in doing.

Once a year I'd invite a lot of other old maids to my place for a day.

I'd eat real healthy things, like fruit and vegetables.

I'd have fun being an old maid.

—Grade 8, Age 13, Pennsylvania
(Blackboard Bulletin)

Garden Patch. c. 1900–20. Wool. 31 × 32. LaGrange Co., Indiana. Faye and Don Walters. An unusual pattern employs the colors and workmanship common to Amish quilts.

Nine-Patch, c. 1885. Cotton, 31 × 38. Holmes Co., Ohio. Sandra Mitchell. The simple beauty of this quilt is accented by its use of only one color in varying shades.

Winter

Winter

Ben said I was just plain dumb to stay outside so long when it was so cold but I didn't want to stop skating. It was the first day of good ice and I didn't want to leave early or walk home alone. But when Ike hit the bank playing crack-the-whip, it sorta put a damper on things. His ankle got fat and he said it just didn't feel right. That's when we decided to call it quits. I'll tell you, when we finally got home, those Christmas cookies sure tasted good. Especially when you dunked them in piping hot cocoa.

I can hardly believe Christmas is only two weeks away. Mama says none of us are allowed in the spare room. That's where she has the gifts hidden. We children always pull names. I got Levi's again this year. Had it last year too. That's when Ben got me a big fat activity book with dot-to-dots, mazes, fill-in-the-blanks, and stuff. Levi got Sara a doily for her hope chest and Sara got Jonas some extra heavy socks for when he goes trapping. Can't remember what Leah and Ben got. Mama and Daddy always get each of us children something and they get each other something too. Last year Daddy got Mama a bigger canner and she got him an extension ladder. We hung that same old construction paper chain in the doorway again between the two front rooms. I just should have made a new one last year instead of fixing it after Levi and Ben were rowdying around and tore it. A couple of years ago, Ebersoles gave us a fruit basket for Christmas when they came to get eggs. It had some bells on a stick stuck in it. Ben broke the stick off and I hung the bells on the china closet door knob last week. Now the decorating is done.

I always think Second Christmas is as much fun as Christmas Day itself. Having two holidays in a row sure is special. We always take turns having all Mama's brothers and sisters one year for Second Christmas, and Daddy's the next. Last year we went sledding back on Zook's hill. Susie and I hid behind some of the trees and chucked snowballs when people sledded by. I broke David B.'s glasses and Daddy said I had to help pay the bill to get them fixed! It made me cross.

We've been practicing for the Christmas program at school. We're doing a play that uses people for everything including the furniture. Naomi and I are a rocking chair and Ben and Ike are a table. One day in practice, Joe sat up too high on Naomi and me and smashed the chair right into the table. Teacher said there are a lot of spots that need brushing up on before all the parents come. We know what she means.

The school room stinks these days after recess. When we all come in from playing in the snow we pile our mittens on the stove to dry them. Then the air gets sorta steamy. I always think it smells like wet dogs.

Teacher promised that we could go for a sleigh ride tomorrow afternoon. We're going over to Beiler School to Christmas carol for them. They were at our school last Tuesday. So now it's our turn. The biggest surprise of all will be having a fruit and can roll for their teacher. Levi said he's going to roll eggs. But he knows he better not.

The boys are taking off school tomorrow to go to the horse auction. It's different than the usual Tuesday sales. Lots of horses and mules coming from out of state will be there. I still wish I could go but Daddy says the boys will have more use for what they will learn from going than I will. So it's off to school for me.

Daddy's been on the lookout for another driving horse. Ever since Star took a notion to cut the corner short and whammed the buggy into the corn crib, Daddy says she's been favoring her right side. He's afraid it's just going to go downhill since Star's almost 14, so we're going to have to start thinking about doing something soon. I don't re-

Amish life is not a cold and frozen existence. There is a sense of belonging. There is mutual caring and sharing that provides warmth for its numbers despite the temperatures around them.

member when we took old Jack to the auction for the last time. Mama and Daddy both said he was such a gentle old horse, but everybody's time comes sooner or later.

I went up to the attic for another bologna this afternoon. That's our third one since we smoked them in the fall and took them upstairs. Each one is less squishey and tougher than the last. When we finally bring the last one down in late spring it'll be as tough as shoes. Leah says they get so dried out we could use them for shoe soles and they'd outlast the uppers!

Yesterday Daddy said from the looks of things, it'll probably be about four weeks till tobacco is ready to strip. Those are always fun evenings. We get the stove all fired up. I'll never forget the time the stove pipe got so hot it got red. Somebody is always telling stories or jokes. And the smell is always so funny—terrible dirty, sweet and musty all at once.

Christmas sure will be different without Groossmammi. She always came over when we baked Christmas cookies. Her favorite cookie cutter was a star with a tiny scalloped edge. We liked to sprinkle red sugar and peanuts on top and bake them till they were just turning brown around the edges. We made a lot of those stars this year. Whenever we eat them we think of all the happy days with Groossmammi. Daadi comes over more often since she's gone. He says we children are a comfort for him.

Mama and us girls finished the quilt Groossmammi started. She had it all done except for the binding. Mama said we'll keep it as a Sunday quilt.

Star. c. 1930. Wool. 27 × 30. Ohio. Nancy Glazer. Quilting designs in the four corners surrounding the star echo the diamond pattern of the pieced design.

Tumbling Blocks. c. 1935–40. Rayon and cotton. 37 × 41. Mifflin Co., Pennsylvania. Private collection. Skillful use of color creates the illusion of three-dimensional cubes. With further study six-pointed stars also appear.

Variable Star, c. 1920. Cotton, 33 × 38. Holmes Co., Ohio. Sandra Mitchell. Lighter fabric on several of the star points produces a twinkling effect. Bright red binding adds to the dazzle.

Thoughts of a Five-Year-Old

Our 5-year-old gets bored sometimes
Since brother is in school.
When the days are blustery out
He's in here as a rule.

Sometimes he plays so nicely
With toy animals and such.
And sometimes he just daydreams
And doesn't do too much.

As he goes about his play
He's sometimes deep in thought.
Here are some of the questions
His little mind has wrought.

"If the moon is down at Bens,"
He asked of me one day.
"Can Isaiahs see it?"
(Seven hundred miles away.)

One day we talked about the bears
"They hibernate," I said.
"If someone shot a sleeping bear,
Would he know he's dead?"

I guess his thoughts were once at church
When we at the table sat,

He asked, "How do the men know
Which one is their hat?"

He thinks about the factories
"How do they make the toys?
And wieners, and some other things
Tempting to little boys."

"How do people make furniture?"
And, "How does God make wood?"
Sometimes I cannot answer him,
Like I wish I could.

"Why do we need thumbs?" he asked
And, "Do our fingers grow?"
He thought he'd like to watch them,
Though it happens much too slow.

"How do the people make the roads
For the cars and trucks and bus?"
"Why do cows have four legs?"
Perhaps he compared with us.

"How does Daddy know it's morning?"
All the family's sleeping good.
Yet he faithfully gets up,
Every morning when he should.

(Family Life)

From outside, the Amish community sometimes appears postcard perfect. But they too have problems. Perhaps one of their greatest struggles is knowing how to maintain a balance between two values they strive to embody: perfection and humility.

Rolling Stone, 1925. Wool, 42 × 50. LaGrange Co., Indiana. Pat and Kemp Beall. Although the pattern consists of triangles and squares, each patch appears rounded. Quilting is generous overall.

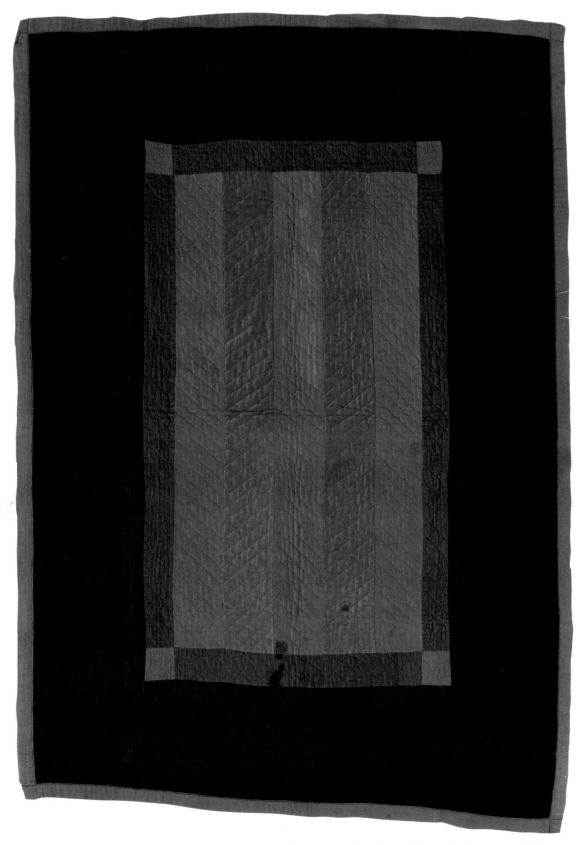

Bars, c. 1910–15. Wool, 41 × 58. Lancaster Co., Pennsylvania. Ron and Marilyn Kowaleski, Grant Street Antiques, Lancaster, PA. Simplicity in both pieced pattern and quilting designs characterize this quilt.

Bars variation, c. 1940. Cotton, 27 × 38. Holmes Co., Ohio. Collection of Eve and David Wheatcroft, Lewisburg, PA. A new rendition of the more common Bars pattern, this one experiments with several borders.

Amish children have fewer vocational options than many of their non-Amish peers. And yet these are probably some of the most secure, contented, and happy children in American society.

Winter

If God allows strength, health and ability I wish to help and work willingly. When the men are in need of help, I would try to assist them. Perhaps they want to get their plowing done or their corn cut, or even crop seeding. I would try to do the milking and their other necessary chores in the barn voluntarily. As for in the house, I trust to have a good talent at baking, cooking, canning, and sewing.

I hope to be kind, trustworthy, helpful and religious. Also I want to be bashful, for I want to try not to be outstanding and loud like some people are—not that I mean I am more than other people, either.

I also want to be aware of nature's creations of birds, flowers, and scenery at all times, but mostly in my spare time, if I have any.

—Grade 8, Age 13, Ontario
(Blackboard Bulletin)

Railroad Crossing, c. 1915. Cotton and Wool, 43 × 50. Holmes Co., Ohio. Scott and Cindy Albright. Crossings are clearly defined and offset by tiny brightly colored triangles. The stars in the center of each patch serve as a focal point.

Diamonds and Squares. 1930. Cotton and cotton sateen. 30 × 38. Holmes Co., Ohio. Private Collection. Squares and diamonds seem to be floating in the interior space. The black border keeps all in bounds.

Center Diamond, c. 1940–45. Cotton and rayon. 48 × 48. Mifflin Co., Pennsylvania. Private Collection. The outer border of this quilt appears to be fabric recycled from a dress. Fade lines follow the folds of a pleated skirt.

Plain Quilt, 1890. Cotton, 28 × 38. Holmes Co., Ohio. Scott and Cindy Albright. A pair of exquisite feather wreaths are surrounded by a narrow inner border. The outer border is quilted with groups of diagonal lines.

Most Amish children walk to school. When school buses can't get through and classes are cancelled elsewhere, Amish school goes on. Children bring their sleds to take advantage of the snow-covered roads during recess.

A Lesson I'll Always Remember

One evening this winter I made a mistake I'll never forget. It was getting dark so Dad sent me in the house to light the lanterns. When the lanterns were lighted I blew out the match and laid it on a pasteboard box.

I went out to help chore when all of a sudden my sister came out telling that a pasteboard box is burning in the house. So Dad and I ran quickly to see how serious it was. There in front of the house was the box full with expensive calf medicine which Dad had bought that day. As I was cleaning up the mess I thought to myself after this I have to cool the match before I leave.

—Grade 6, Indiana
(Blackboard Bulletin)

Most Amish schools have all eight grades together in one room with one teacher. Religion is not taught in school, for the Amish believe that training in faith is the responsibility of the family and church.

In the Teacher's Place

One morning when we arrived at school most of the children were there but the teacher was missing. It was already past time to start school and someone suggested we just start without the teacher and being I was the oldest I was assigned the teacher's job. Everything went fine except several of the younger boys didn't want to come in. Finally after some coaxing we got them persuaded to come in.

Around recess time our teacher finally arrived. She had missed the bus which she usually came with and not knowing the bus had already left she waited for the bus. When the bus didn't show up for a long time she decided to bring the buggy.

I really enjoyed that short while of teaching, mostly because the others all tried their best. This taught me that teaching would be more enjoyable for my teacher, too, if I would always try my best.

—Grade 8, Missouri
(Blackboard Bulletin)

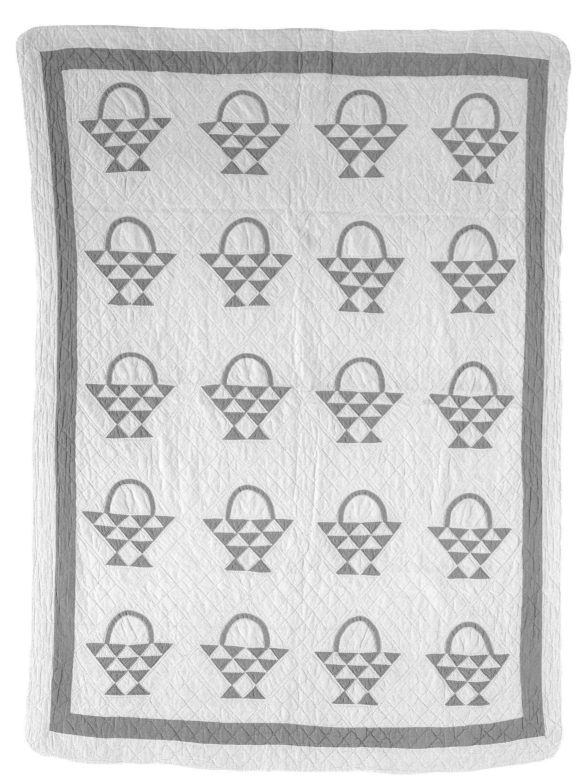

Baskets, c. 1930. Cotton. 36 × 49. LaGrange Co., Indiana. Pat and Kemp Beall. Both pattern and color make this unusual among Amish quilts.

Reading and Sources

Cross Reference

Pellman, Rachel T. *Small Amish Quilt Patterns*. Intercourse, Pennsylvania: Good Books, 1985.

About Antique Amish Quilts

Bishop, Robert and Elizabeth Safanda. *A Gallery of Amish Quilts*. New York: E. P. Dutton and Company, Inc., 1976.

Haders, Phyllis. *Sunshine and Shadow: The Amish and Their Quilts*. New York: Universe Books, 1976.

Horton, Roberta. *Amish Adventure*. Lafayette, California: C & T Publishing, 1983.

Lawson, Suzy. *Amish Inspiration*. Cottage Grove, Oregon: Amity Publications, 1982.

Pellman, Rachel T. *Amish Quilt Patterns*. Intercourse, Pennsylvania: Good Books, 1984.

————, and Kenneth Pellman. *The World of Amish Quilts*. Intercourse, Pennsylvania: Good Books, 1984.

About Other Quilts

Beyer, Jinny. *Patchwork Patterns*. McLean, Virginia: EPM Publications, 1979.

Binney, Edwin, 3rd and Gail Binney-Winslow. *Homage to Amanda*. San Francisco: R K Press, 1984.

Bonesteel, Georgia. *More Lap Quilting with Georgia Bonesteel*. Birmingham, Alabama: Oxmoor House, Inc., 1985.

Danneman, Barbara. *Step by Step Quiltmaking*. New York: Western Publishing Company, Inc., 1975.

Finley, Ruth E. *Old Patchwork Quilts and the Women Who Made Them*. New York: Charles T. Branford Company, 1929.

Fox, Sandi. *Small Endearments: 19th Century Quilts for Children and Dolls*. Los Angeles: The Los Angeles Municipal Art Gallery Associates, 1980.

Garoutte, Sally, ed. *Uncoverings 1980*. Mill Valley, California: American Quilt Study Group, 1981.

————. *Uncoverings 1982*. Mill Valley, California: American Quilt Study Group, 1983.

Haders, Phyllis. *The Warner Collector's Guide to American Quilts*. New York: The Main Street Press, 1981.

Hall, Carrie A. And Rose G. Kretsinger. *The Romance of the Patchwork Quilt in America*. New York: Bonanza Books, 1935.

Hassel, Carla J. *You Can Be A Super Quilter!* Des Moines, Iowa: Wallace-Homestead Book Company, 1980.

Holstein, Jonathon. *The Pieced Quilt: An American Design Tradition*. Boston: New York Graphic Society, 1973.

Houck, Carter and Myron Miller. *American Quilts and How To Make Them*. New York: Charles Scribner's Sons, 1975.

Johnson, Bruce. *A Child's Comfort: Baby and Doll Quilts in American Folk Art*. New York: The Museum of American Folk Art, 1977.

Khin, Yvonne M. *The Collector's Dictionary of Quilt Names and Patterns*. Washington, D.C.: Acropolis Books, Ltd., 1980.

Kiracofe, Roderick and Michael Kile. *The Quilt Digest*. San Francisco: Kiracofe and Kile, 1983.

————. *The Quilt Digest*. San Francisco: Kiracofe and Kile, 1984.

Leone, Diana. *The Sampler Quilt*. Santa Clara, California: Leone Publications, 1980.

McCloskey, Marsha. *Wall Quilts*. Bothell, Washington: That Patchwork Place, 1983.

Murwin, Susan Aylsworth and Suzzy Chalfant Payne. *Quick and Easy Patchwork on the Sewing Machine*. New York: Dover Publications, Inc., 1979.

Orlovsky, Patsy, and Myron Orlovsky. *Quilts in America*. New York: McGraw Hill Book Company, 1974.

Pellman, Rachel T. and Joanne Ranck. *Quilts Among the Plain People*. Intercourse, Pennsylvania: Good Books, 1981.

Tomlonson, Judy Schroeder. *Mennonite Quilts and Pieces*. Intercourse, Pennsylvania: Good Books, 1985.

Woodard, Thos. K. and Blanche Greenstein. *Crib Quilts and Other Small Wonders*. New York: E. P. Dutton, 1981.

About the Amish

Amish Cooking. Aylmer, Ontario: Pathway Publishing House, 1965.

Bender, H. S. *The Anabaptist Vision*. Scottdale, Pennsylvania: Herald Press, 1967.

Braght, Thieleman J. van, Comp. *The Bloody Theatre; or, Martyrs Mirror*. Scottdale, Pennsylvania, 1951.

Budget, The. Sugarcreek, Ohio, 1890. A weekly newspaper serving the Amish and Mennonite communities.

Devoted Christian's Prayer Book. Aylmer, Ontario: Pathway Publishing House, 1967.

Family Life. Amish periodical published monthly. Aylmer, Ontario: Pathway Publishing House.

Fisher, Sara and Rachel Stahl. *The Amish School*. Intercourse, Pennsylvania: Good Books, 1985.

Gingerich, Orland. *The Amish of Canada*. Waterloo, Ontario: Conrad Press, 1972.

Good, Merle. *Who Are the Amish?* Intercourse, Pennsylvania: Good Books, 1985.

——— , and Phyllis Pellman Good. *20 Most Asked Questions about the Amish and Mennonites*. Intercourse, Pennsylvania: Good Books, 1979.

Good, Phyllis Pellman and Rachel Thomas Pellman. *From Amish and Mennonite Kitchens*. Intercourse, Pennsylvania: Good Books, 1984.

Hostetler, John A. *Amish Life*. Scottdale, Pennsylvania: Herald Press, 1959.

——— . *Amish Society*. Baltimore, Maryland: John Hopkins University Press, 1963.

Hostetler, John A. and Gertrude E. Huntingdon. *Children in Amish Society*. New York: Holt, Rinehart and Winston, Inc., 1971.

Keim, Albert N. *Compulsory Education and the Amish*. Boston: Beacon Press, 1975.

Klaassen, Walter. *Anabaptism: Neither Catholic nor Protestant*. Waterloo, Ontario: Conrad Press, 1972.

Ruth, John L. *A Quiet and Peaceable Life*. Intercourse, Pennsylvania: Good Books, 1979.

Scott, Stephen. *Plain Buggies*. Intercourse, Pennsylvania: Good Books, 1981.

——— . *Why Do They Dress That Way?* Intercourse, Pennsylvania: Good Books, 1985.

Crazy Ann, c. 1920. Cotton. 42 × 66. Indiana or Ohio. Rebecca Haarer. One white triangle wandered into the plan of this turbulent pattern.

Index

About the Authors

The Pellmans are well-known as the authors of THE WORLD OF AMISH QUILTS.

Rachel Thomas Pellman is manager of The Old Country Store in Intercourse, Pennsylvania, which features quilts, crafts and toys made by more than 250 Amish and Mennonite craftspersons. A graduate of Eastern Mennonite College, she has written AMISH QUILT PATTERNS and SMALL AMISH QUILT PATTERNS. She has also co-authored QUILTS AMONG THE PLAIN PEOPLE, FROM AMISH AND MENNONITE KITCHENS, and 12 Pennsylvania Dutch Cookbooks.

Kenneth R. Pellman is manager of The People's Place, an educational center concerned with Amish and Mennonite arts, faith and culture. Kenny graduated from Eastern Mennonite College, where he taught drama for one year. His photography appears in several books, including a National Geographic publication. He is currently working on two more manuscripts that deal with Amish and Mennonite themes.

The Pellmans were married in 1976. They live in Lancaster, Pennsylvania with their two young sons, Nathaniel and Jesse. They are members of the Rossmere Mennonite Church.